Simply Summer

GOURMET MEALS MADE DELICIOUSLY EASY
WITH TIPS FOR ELEGANT LIVING

Angela Tunner
THE RENAISSANCE GOURMET

SIMPLY SUMMER
Gourmet Meals Made Deliciously Easy with Tips for Elegant Living
THE RENAISSANCE GOURMET

Author Angela Tunner
Published by Eat Like a Millionaire Omnimedia Inc. Vancouver, BC

EAT LIKE A MILLIONAIRE ™ OMNIMEDIA INC.

Cover photograph by Kevin Clark Photography.
Food styling by David Robertson.
Book design by Jacqueline Wang and George Plumley.
Cover design by Angela Chan Design.
Edited by Wendy Thomas.
Proofread by Lesley Cameron.

PRINTED IN CANADA
10 9 8 7 6 5 4 3 2 1

Library and Archives Canada Cataloguing in Publication

Tunner, Angela, 1967-
Simply summer / Angela Tunner.

Includes index.
ISBN 978-0-9783561-0-1

1. Cookery. 2. Summer. I. Title.

TX715.6.T78 2007   641.5'64   C2007-902949-3

CONTENTS

Read This First • 4

Preface • 6

Acknowledgements • 8

Introduction • 9

Easy Entertaining Tips • 16

Tips for Coping with Summer Heat • 18

The Recipes • 21

Breakfast • 24

Lunch or Light Dinner • 36

Dinner • 48

Dessert • 68

Beverages • 84

Conversions and Measurement Equivalents • 89

Index • 94

Read This First

You're probably used to seeing that command in computer manuals and programs. There's a reason for it—it will make your life easier! Please read this first and you will find you benefit so much more from this book.

The recipes in this book are revolutionary because they rely almost exclusively on no cooking—perfect for summer! This section will introduce you to some No-Cook Cooking concepts that will make the book easy to use.

The principles of No-Cook Cooking

Use fresh ingredients as much as possible. They are not only the key to better eating, they also minimize the cooking factor.

Use the oven as little as possible. Some foods do need to be cooked as they are central to this repertoire of cooking and add immensely to the flavor of the meals. Cook these foods when it is cooler, usually in the morning. However, if you have to cook in the evening, comfort yourself with the knowledge that the house has time to cool down.

Make the most of your blender. Summer soups are not only a great way to cool down, they are also an excellent and elegant way to increase your fruit intake.

Make the most of your toaster oven—actually cook in it! Using often-neglected appliances like the toaster oven is a key concept in this type of meal preparation. A toaster oven that can hold four pieces of bread or a 9-inch pie plate is ideal. I also highly recommend a convection toaster oven for getting the best-quality baking and cooking. You will find you use your regular oven far less often year round, not just in the summer.

Make the most of your microwave—actually cook in it too! The microwave is an excellent kitchen tool and one I could not do without in my kitchen. Be sure to get a really good one. See Microwaves, below, for usage and safety guidelines, with tips from a microwave expert.

Reduce your trips to the store by bulk buying. Bulk buying does double duty. It saves you time and reduces the number of trips you make in your car. Just because stores are open at all hours does not mean you should shop more frequently. Imagine how much more time you'll have for other things, and you're less likely to run out of supplies when you have a well-provisioned cupboard.

Have a feeling of abundance where your cooking/no cooking is concerned. One of the keys to eating like a millionaire and feeling good about your food is abundance. Salads heaped in a bowl look impressive (use a smaller bowl to create that feel). Abundance is not about gluttony or overstuffing, however, it is about creating a sense of lushness and fullness.

Use supermarket shortcuts like pre-cooked meats and cakes. I'm not referring to pre-packaged foods but to those foods that are already cooked for us, thus reducing our cooking workload and turning meal preparation times more into meal assembly times. Choose these foods for quality and excellence. In these recipes I'll introduce you to some simple ways to cut corners—without cutting down on quality—by using rotisserie chickens, smoked hams, chicken stock, packaged pasta, sliced meats, canned custards and puddings, and bakery goods such as angel food cakes and pound cakes, which can be turned into elegant and easy desserts, for example. Remember: Quality not quantity is what is important.

Choose your supermarket shortcuts wisely and for quality. Quality is the Renaissance way!

Keep it simple. Keep it elegant.

Keep it fresh. Fresh food is better for your health and reduces the need for cooking.

Use local and seasonal fruits and vegetables. Support your local markets and farmers! You will be rewarded with some of the finest, freshest produce you'll ever taste, especially when it's in season!

Eat outdoors as much as possible. Enjoy the summer and outdoors as often as you can before we are all confined inside again during the long, cold, gray months of winter. Enjoy the summer weather and appreciate the beauty of your surroundings. Make your outdoor space beautiful. Make it your oasis! The atmosphere at the table makes a big difference to the dining experience. Too hot? Use a fan to cool down, even on an outdoor patio. Go to just as much trouble preparing the table as you do indoors. What a difference a tablecloth, placemats, and napkins (fabric, not paper!) can make. Even a single blossom in a little vase can dress up a simple setting. As the sun sets, add a few flickering candles or turn on the glittery fairy lights. It's so easy to do, but the payoff is a feeling of indulgence, intimacy, and relaxation.

Preface

It's hot and you're hungry but you're tired of the barbecue. What can you do in the kitchen?

I've never been a big fan of the heat. I remember long, hard summer days when I was cooking in unbearably hot restaurant kitchens. You cooked until you were exhausted and then still had half your shift left to struggle through in the sweltering heat. Once I stopped cooking as a professional, I was done with cooking in the heat! But I still wanted to eat all those delicious fruits and vegetables you see at the markets and I still wanted to prepare the gourmet spreads I am accustomed to for everyday meals. I didn't want to miss the bursts of colors and flavors we can only get in the summer.

When you can prepare delicious and attractive meals with a minimum of fuss and muss, you'll feel more like embracing the summer and all it has to offer. What can you do to get the most from this special season? Read on! I have gathered together many of my own tips and techniques as well as those that my readers have suggested, plus tips from other hot climates on how they cope with the heat.

For the love of good food

The family is one of nature's masterpieces.
George Santayana

The greenness of No-Cook Cooking

I think we are all aware of the changes in our environment but many of us feel overwhelmed by the challenge of slowing down the damage. What difference can one person make? This was what I asked myself after I'd seen Al Gore's movie, *An Inconvenient Truth*. But after some thought, I realized that No-Cook Cooking was, in its way, my contribution to the solution. It may not be a big contribution, but every little bit helps. It helped me feel a little better but I was also more resolved than ever to share my message that you can beat the summer heat, help the environment, and still eat well during hot weather.

The cooking techniques I outline in this book will initiate some subtle changes that will help the environment in your home and the world at large, even if it's just a little. So share the news with your family and friends. No-Cook Cooking is the new, greener way to cook and I am going to give you the tools to make it easier!

Here are some of the ways No-Cook Cooking is green:

- Shopping in bulk saves trips to the store.

- Using your microwave and toaster oven saves on heat and electricity, thereby benefiting the environment at home and the environment at large.

- Using items like rotisserie chicken and pre-cooked meats and fish means one less oven on and less heat generated, but remember to choose prepared foods carefully. The shorter the list of ingredients, the better.

Angela Tunner
The Renaissance Gourmet

Acknowledgements

First, a double thanks to my husband, Greg, for his never-ending support. Thanks for being my sounding board, my voice of reason, and my unwavering traveling companion on this journey. Even as this thing grew so fast you could hardly keep up, you were there for me. Thanks for all the sushi and for your understanding about my many late nights of writing and incessant phone calls. To my son, Cole, who is too young to know that Mommy has written a book, but old enough to understand that Mommy sure was busy a lot. This all started because of you. You are the best distraction whenever I need a break and you inspire me to keep cooking every time you chant, "Yum, more, more, more!" There was many a time you sat on my lap while I wrote then tore about my office when you grew bored with that. I will tell you all about our adventures when you are older.

So many wonderful, gracious, and talented people were involved in the writing of this book. I worked with a huge team of experts and talents from all areas of book publishing whose knowledge and input are directly responsible for many of the books and cookbooks you already know, love, and own. Without their enthusiasm and participation this book would never have happened. First, a huge thank you to Kimberly Plumley, my publicist, who believed in this project from the very start, even when I had written only one chapter. Her tireless efforts to promote my passion were invaluable. Her participation was an integral part of the success of this book, and the friendship we have forged has meant the world to me. Thank you to Wendy Thomas, Therese Parent, Mary Luz Mejia, Jorge Rocha, Holly Moore, Samantha Hoyt, Eric Vanderluit and the team, Bob Lesperance and his team, Dianne Faber, and Angela Chan, Jacqueline Wang, Lesley Cameron, George Plumley, Alexander Boynton, and Mandy Lui. Thanks to Schiffman and Associates, New York, and to Marie T. Smith and Carolyn Dodson. Thank you all a million times, thank you.

Thanks to all the media in North America who allowed me to share my tips and information for making cooking easier with their audiences. I used to work with some of them many moons ago when I worked in radio. It is a little strange being on the other side of the mic!

Thanks to all those wonderful cookbook writers and food television talents who have inspired me. Ina Garten, with her delicious French-inspired meals, is a personal favorite. I thank her for writing my favorite of her cookbooks, *Barefoot in Paris*. Martha Stewart, through Everyday Foods and Martha Stewart Living, has been a continued inspiration to me to add the "good things" to my life.

8

Introduction

Welcome to the heart of the home—the kitchen!

It's summer and it's hot. Who wants to cook? I know I don't. It's my least favorite time of year to cook, so I usually pack up my pots and pans (so to speak) and settle into a new way of cooking.

Typically, my appetite also decreases significantly, and I favor lighter, smaller meals that can be prepared without having to heat up myself or my kitchen. I enjoy barbecues, but I get tired of them day after day. I want to eat the kinds of things that I do during the rest of the year but I want to make them more in tune with the flavors of the season. I'm looking for something quick and elegant, but with little or no oven use. And it definitely has to be gourmet.

In the following pages, I'm going to show you some of the foods I prepare in the summer months to satisfy my demanding requirements while keeping my food budget within bounds and still producing enjoyable, flavorful, and elegant meals.

You'll be introduced to dishes like Gourmet Dinner Salad (page 50) made with artichokes, goat cheese, pear, and rotisserie chicken; gorgeous Apple Vanilla and Lavender (page 72) cooked in the microwave; succulent Summer Mangos with Nutmeg (page 70) cooked in the toaster oven; Smoked Salmon, Brie, and Balsamic Portobello Mushrooms Baguette (page 42) prepared in the toaster oven; and Cold Melon Soup with Port (page 74) prepared in the blender.

Are you feeling hungry yet? Dive into this guide to good summer eating with The Renaissance Gourmet's *Simply Summer*. The time-saving tips will let you and your family and friends enjoy more time together. *Bon appétit!*

Getting started

The best thing to do when preparing for No-Cook Cooking in the summer is to stock up your kitchen and pantry.

Tools and equipment

Take an inventory before the summer and identify any gaps in your equipment. Do you have good working tools and microwave-safe dishes for cooking? Do you need to replace any of your appliances? Prepare now, and save time later.

Here are the basic tools and equipment I'll refer to over and over in the recipes in the following pages:

Baskets	Outdoor dishware
Blender	Ovenproof dishes
Cutting boards	Paring knife
Knives	Serving spoons
Melon baller	Silicone microwave lids
Microwave	Toaster oven
Microwave-proof dishes	Wooden spoons
Napkins	

Microwaves: What you need to know

Microwaves have come a long way over the past 20 or 30 years. They are much more powerful now, and so they cook even faster. Their speed also makes them far more economical, and of course, like other technology, they have become lighter since they can now be made with smaller and lighter parts.

They are also much safer than they used to be, but remember that safety also depends on knowledge and careful use. An item is only as safe as the way it is operated. Always take care, take time, and stay alert to make sure you are using your microwave with safety in mind. Be sure your appliance is in good working order. If it's very old or has had a fire in it, it's time to replace it. To make an informed choice when you go out shopping for a replacement, read the tips below. Be sure to dispose of your old microwave with care. Check with your municipality to see if there is a special disposal method in your area.

Safe microwave use

The great thing about microwaves is that they heat fast, cook fast, use less energy, and don't heat up the kitchen! But as with any appliance, there are some safety precautions you should take.

- Don't use colored or soft plastics as they could melt, especially when used with foods that contain fats, like gravy. Always use microwave-safe dishes.

- Always use oven mitts to remove hot items. Sometimes the dish can get very hot. It is an oven, remember. Always play it safe.

- Don't use plastic wrap, especially when steaming or cooking for longer periods of time (3 minutes or more). Plastic wrap is not designed for heating. It is designed as a barrier for refrigerator storage.

- When steaming foods like vegetables, cover the dish with a silicone lid and wear gloves to remove the dish, cover and all, from the microwave. Once the dish is on the counter, carefully remove the silicone cover to release the steam.

Looking for a new microwave?

- Look for a microwave with about 1000 watts (the power of a microwave is measured in watts). This level of power will ensure good cooking. Generally the higher the wattage, the more quickly the food will cook.

- Look for models with features such as Sensor Cook and Sensor Reheat, which can be found on the Panasonic Genius brand. Such features take the guesswork out of microwave cooking, making it quite literally as easy as pressing a button.

- Make sure the oven has a revolving tray for more even cooking.

Tips for microwave cooking

- The microwave is great for steaming or wet cooking. Again, use a microwave-safe container and top it with a silicone cover.

- When defrosting frozen meats and fish, submerge the packages completely in water before putting them in the microwave on Defrost.

Stocking the pantry in summer

Here is a list of the items that will make No-Cook Cooking a breeze. Make a copy of this page and take it with you to the market. Shopping from a list not only saves time, it also makes shopping and cooking much easier.

Fruit

- ☐ Apples
- ☐ Oranges
- ☐ Lemons
- ☐ Limes
- ☐ Watermelon
- ☐ Cantaloupe
- ☐ Peaches
- ☐ Pears
- ☐ Mangos
- ☐ Kiwis
- ☐ Bananas
- ☐ Blueberries
- ☐ Cherries
- ☐ Strawberries

Bakery

- ☐ Croissants (butter or chocolate)
- ☐ Pound cake or angel food cake
- ☐ Baguette
- ☐ Bakery bread

Vegetables and fresh herbs

- ☐ Zucchini
- ☐ Tomatoes (Roma and cherry)
- ☐ Green beans
- ☐ Mushrooms
- ☐ Portobello mushrooms
- ☐ English cucumber
- ☐ Spinach leaves
- ☐ Fennel
- ☐ Belgian endive
- ☐ Butter lettuce
- ☐ Mixed baby greens
- ☐ Potatoes
- ☐ Creamer or white potatoes
- ☐ Asparagus
- ☐ Onions
- ☐ Italian parsley
- ☐ Mint leaves
- ☐ Chives

Pantry staples

- ☐ Balsamic vinegar
- ☐ White wine vinegar
- ☐ Red wine vinegar
- ☐ Pear vinegar (by Vilux)
- ☐ Olive oil
- ☐ Dijon mustard
- ☐ Mango chutney
- ☐ Honey
- ☐ Vanilla extract
- ☐ Vanilla bean
- ☐ Cinnamon
- ☐ Nutmeg
- ☐ Tarragon, dried
- ☐ Chives, dried
- ☐ Sea salt
- ☐ Pepper (ground or peppercorns)
- ☐ Canned custard
- ☐ Sherry
- ☐ Port
- ☐ Fig or apricot jam
- ☐ Almonds, slivered
- ☐ Pistachios
- ☐ Pecans
- ☐ Olives
- ☐ Capers
- ☐ Artichoke hearts, jarred, in oil
- ☐ Canned tuna
- ☐ Chickpeas, canned
- ☐ White beans, canned
- ☐ Kidney beans
- ☐ Coconut, sweetened
- ☐ Cocoa
- ☐ Brown sugar
- ☐ Granulated sugar
- ☐ Pasta
- ☐ Lavender flowers

Fridge staples

- ☐ Whipping cream
- ☐ Mayonnaise
- ☐ Lemon juice
- ☐ Yogurt
- ☐ Rotisserie chicken
- ☐ Honey ham, sliced
- ☐ Prosciutto
- ☐ Smoked salmon
- ☐ Parmesan cheese
- ☐ Brie
- ☐ Mascarpone
- ☐ Swiss cheese
- ☐ Goat cheese
- ☐ Eggs
- ☐ Butter
- ☐ Pasta, fresh

Freezer staples

- ☐ Ice cream
- ☐ Sorbet
- ☐ Pie crust, deep dish

With these basics on hand, you'll be ready to whip up an impressive meal in short order and still be cool, calm, and collected.

Tips to make shopping and mealtimes easier

Don't panic when it's time to replenish the pantry or fridge. The heat sometimes makes me feel as if my brain has stopped working, so I've come up with a system that makes shopping on hot days a lot easier. It all starts with my shopping list and my baskets.

- Pre-print your shopping list. If you keep the list of basic pantry, fridge, and freezer staples on your computer or keep several photocopies on hand, you can easily run your eye down it and cross off anything that doesn't need replacing. Always shop from a list!

- Keep your shopping baskets or bags by the door. Treat yourself to beautiful and practical shopping baskets. Look for a pretty cloth bag or a woven basket. They're easier to carry and better for the environment.

- Place the shopping list in the basket, ready to go. You'll never forget your list again!

- Keep bins in the car. These practical containers make carrying your items into the house easier. They save trips back and forth to the car and items won't roll around in the car while you're driving. They're especially useful if you've been shopping in a variety of stores.

- Don't forget to have fun when food shopping. When you go to the market, stop for a moment to appreciate the beauty of the colors and scents around you. What a bounty of food! Take a breath and take it all in.

After the shopping is over

If you do need to cook anything, it's worth remembering that the house is often cooler in the morning. This is a great time to make balsamic onions, compotes, and other cooked items. Making them in bulk also means you will be cooking less often.

- Make things in advance—plates of sandwiches, veggie and fruit dishes, for example. This type of preparation makes the food more accessible to your family and cuts down on mealtime cooking. Cooking ahead turns meal preparation into a fast and easy assembly job. By cooking this way, you'll halve the time you spend on meal preparation. A little piggybacking during meal preparation saves a lot of work later.

- Always having meals on hand is helpful if power outages occur because of summer storms. You'll have foods that are all ready to eat! Just remember to avoid opening and closing your fridge too much during those power outages!

- When you have fruits and vegetables prepared, your family is more likely to grab them instead of a processed snack. Processed food can be helpful in the summer but you don't want to rely on it too much. It's just as important to keep nutrition in mind in the summer as it is in the winter.

Saving time should not mean sacrificing quality! Choose carefully.

Easy Entertaining Tips

The outdoor eating basket

This is the time of year for casual and relaxed. Eating outside can add a challenge to the dining process, though, as you might have to move your table settings outdoors. Here are some of the things I do to save multiple trips and to make it easier to eat outside. Create your own outdoor eating basket and setting the table outdoors will be instantly easier!

- Gather together what you use outdoors and keep it in one spot—a basket or bin that can be easily transported in and out, for example. Think of it as a picnic basket of sorts! Fill it with everything you need so you're ready to go for your outdoor meals. Include cutlery, napkins, drinking glasses, placemats, or a tablecloth. Have a separate basket or bin to carry in the dirty dishes. Once the dishes, glasses, cutlery, and other items have been cleaned, put them back in the "picnic basket."

- Use tableware meant specifically for outdoors. It should be tough and durable but that doesn't mean it has to be unattractive. You can find a lovely selection of glass and dishware designed for the rigors and challenges of eating outdoors. Keep your good china for indoor dining. Nothing sounds worse than hearing your grandmother's tea cups shattering on the patio stones!

- Use a cutlery caddy to hold napkins as well. Cutlery, including the napkins, can be placed in the center of the table, secured so as not to blow away but accessible so people can help themselves.

Tips for setting the table for summer dining

🌿 Choose a soft color scheme. Let the colors of the outside take center stage, and keep your table simple but not minimalist. While summer is a time for bright colors, for dining I lean toward a more muted palette of natural colors, like pale blues, browns, greens, and yellows.

🌿 Lighting is an important element in setting a mood. I prefer battery-operated lights for safety and convenience. You can buy lovely tea lights that run on batteries. Set them in clear or frosted votive holders, just as you do with regular tea lights. The wind won't blow them out and they won't create a mess. Use several on a table for a dazzling display.

🌿 Use placemats or tablecloths that are easy to clean off. Because dining outdoors with children is often more relaxed, there are often more accidents too. Wind can be a problem with lightweight fabrics, so always be prepared to improvise if you're entertaining more formally. Tablecloth clips will hold the cloth in place so the ends won't blow up during your meal. Check out dollar stores or kitchen shops for these handy gadgets. Move the table to a more protected or private corner of the patio or arrange tall plants to act as windbreaks.

🌿 Pay attention to luxurious details, like making sure your seating is comfortable. Put seat cushions on hard chairs to give them a more comfortable feel so your guests will enjoy lingering at the table.

🌿 Don't forget flowers! Even a few little vases of simple garden blossoms can add a lot to your table. Fresh is best. Celebrate the season!

Tips for Coping with Summer Heat

I have lived on both coasts and have survived the heat, both dry and humid. Here are some of my tips for beating the summer heat.

Hot tips for keeping cool

- Set a moving fan behind a moving water fountain or bowl of ice.

- Keep a spray bottle filled with spring water and lavender oil handy to keep you cool. Spray a bit on the inside of your elbows, the back of your neck, and behind your knees when you're feeling hot. As the water evaporates, it cools your body.

- Sprinkle bedsheets with non-talc baby powder before climbing into bed.

- Like to work out? Do it in the morning while it's still cool. Moving keeps you warmed up. Lie around for optimum cool!

- Close your blinds and drapes to keep your house cool. Use fans to circulate the air.

- Use an electric or hand-held fan instead of air conditioning to keep cool. Stay as still as you can—just think of those graceful Southern belles, languidly moving a delicate fan in a lily-white hand!

- Keep a pitcher of flavored water in the fridge to sip on. The addition of fresh lemon or lime slices makes the water much more refreshing and delicious.

- Wear breathable fabrics. Manmade fabrics do not breathe like cottons and linen do. Loose tunics, skirts, and pants will keep you cooler and more comfortable.

Cool tips from my readers

I asked members of my foodie community across North America, "What do you do to keep cool in the summer heat?"

Here are six tips.

To keep cool in the summer heat I run cool water over my wrists. Works like a charm every time!

—Celine, St. Catharines, Ontario

In the winter gather up some snow and make snowballs. Put them in your freezer and in the high heat of the season have a snowball fight! Lots of fun and a great way to cool down.

—Kim in Kitimat, B.C.

I live in an apartment, high up. Heat rises, so if it is a real scorcher, I'll wrap six to seven ice cubes in a row in a tea towel and wrap it around my neck for an instant cool down.

—Shirley Scott, Burnaby, B.C.

I make popsicles for my family from pure juice and keep them on hand for those unbearable days. At least when cooling down, I know they are eating a healthier popsicle.

—Anne Davis, Seattle, Washington

I run a few washcloths under cold water and apply them to the back of my neck and on my thighs or stomach. For an extra cold blast, I sit with the cloths on me in front of a fan. Nothing is more refreshing than that!

—Mona Drexell, New York, New York

I love to wear linen and this fabric is the best at keeping me cool. I choose pieces that are billowy and don't sit snugly, so the air circulates and keeps me cool.

—Jan Davidson, Vancouver, B.C.

Luxuriously cool lounging

I have been dubbed the "queen of luxury" by my husband. At any given moment, I can be found making myself super-comfortable and surrounded by as much beauty as possible. I put extra pillows on couches and even have a couch in the kitchen. A phone, my book, a cool beverage with fresh fruit in it, a beautifully presented snack, and a vase of flowers—these are things I like surrounding myself with.

For a luxurious stretch of hot weather lounging, follow the recipe below. Whether it's for 20 minutes or two hours, you'll feel pampered and cooler.

- Find a comfortable spot where the setting is just right—that perfect spot in the garden, or in your home facing a beautiful view, perhaps looking out the window at a favorite tree...

- Set up your space with things that will cool you down. The best thing is an electric fan and a water fountain placed in front of it or a bowl of ice. The air coming off it will be much cooler. Create a spa feel by adding 10 to 15 drops of essential lavender oil for a bit of aromatherapy.

- Set up the fan so that it's facing in the direction of your chair or lounger. Cover the chair or lounger with a cotton sheet—the barrier and its absorption capabilities make the seat much more comfortable.

- Fill a spray bottle with fresh water and maybe a few drops of your favorite essential oil—lavender is always refreshing and sweet orange is good for the skin—then spritz it on your skin when you need some extra cooling.

- Place a small table with iced drinks and a book or magazines, your phone, whatever you need to feel happy, next to your chair.

- Put a few cool snacks like fresh fruit on the table too.

- Relax and enjoy!

The Recipes

These menu plans are based on how I serve the dishes in my home but you can, of course, use each recipe on its own or create your own menu plans. If you are an inexperienced cook or busy parent, the plans will help to take the guesswork and challenge out of planning meals for your family and guests. All the recipes complement one another so it's difficult to get it wrong. Just remember the Rule of Four Flavors, explained below, and it should all turn out beautifully.

The Rule of Four Flavors

The Rule of Four Flavors is based on the concept that every meal should be made up of four complementary flavors or elements. Although you may not realize it, you probably already design a meal in the traditional way—protein, potatoes (or another starchy food), and vegetables. But if you add a fourth item, you take that meal up a level and with relatively little effort on your part!

Ideally, this fourth item or flavor is something unexpected like a condiment, compotes, or preserves. But it could be an extra vegetable or a dollop of mustard. Whatever you choose, the extra element will make your palate jump from flavor to flavor, keeping the meal interesting and leaving you wanting more. Whether it is a fourth flavor in a sandwich or a fourth item on a plate, the Rule of Four Flavors has a magical effect on the experience of eating.

About the recipes

I love repertoire-building recipes. They are like the little black dress for your kitchen. Indispensable, always a good standby, and always in style. The recipes I have included here are neither trendy nor dated. Rather, they are standard recipes built from my trusted kitchen staples with a bit of zing added to keep them new. These new classic recipes and the Renaissance Gourmet way of cooking are elegant, easy, and consistent. They are successful because the main ingredients are carefully chosen to work together to make an unforgettable dish.

About the ingredients

The ingredients you'll be using in these recipes are no farther away than your supermarket and farmers' markets. Flavor is king—simple yet complex bodies of flavors. The look follows close behind—rustic and yet elegant. My philosophy of food preparation and presentation can be summed up in a simple example: It is the difference between plain and ordinary and gourmet and memorable. Creating a gourmet meal is not hard, but how you combine the flavors, colors, and textures of your ingredients will make each meal one your family will remember and ask for again and again.

About make ahead items

Making items ahead of time is one of the cornerstones of good food-preparation practices in professional kitchens. This type of preparation, or prep as it is called, allows restaurants to serve you tasty meals quickly. There's no reason home cooks can't use this technique too. By preparing the make-ahead dishes in this book, you can save time, create lovely flavorful meals, and add complexity to your dishes. A dish is considered a "make ahead" when it can be made in quantity hours or even days ahead. These make ahead dishes are versatile and will have uses in other recipes than the ones they are attached to. Look for the words MAKE AHEAD in the recipes for those items you can make ahead!

Let's see just how simple it is.

Breakfast

About breakfasts

Breakfast is, as the word implies, the breaking from the fast of sleep, and is the first meal we eat after we wake up. In the past, when many people worked in physically demanding jobs, breakfast was the largest meal of the day and was designed to give people energy for most of the day. Now that fewer people are involved in occupations such as agriculture, breakfast has become a neglected meal. It's time that we reclaimed it! Not only is it good for your health, but the morning is also a wonderful time of the day to give something back to yourself, and a small, tasty meal will start the day off on the right foot. Set the mood for your day by putting aside enough time for a good breakfast.

Breakfast can take many forms, and the good news is that there are many options. Whether you're looking for something fast or something more leisurely, the suggestions for summer breakfasts should satisfy you. Since we typically eat less in the summer months, these are light and refreshing dishes designed with the heat and a smaller appetite in mind. You can always have more if you are hungrier.

A great place to get ideas for summer breakfasts is to look at countries with warmer climates. What do they eat to get the day started?

In Australia, breakfast resembles the typical warmer-weather Western breakfast—cereals, toast, fruit, and juices are favored over cooked foods.

In the Mediterranean, the lighter breakfast tradition is what we call a continental breakfast. This breakfast is designed as a light start to the day to hold you over until lunch. In France, Italy, Greece, and Spain, you'll find beverages such as coffee, juice, and milk, and sweet cakes such as pastries or brioche served with jam or cream, or even filled with chocolate. Slices of cold ham or salami, cheese, yogurt, or cereals are also favored.

Here are some gourmet twists on the continental breakfast.

Enjoy!

Citrus Mango Almond Salad

*I love fresh fruit salads, especially when they're teamed with nuts.
This salad makes a wonderful addition to your summer cooking repertoire.
You can serve it for breakfast with a bit of yogurt or with an added
dollop of whipped cream or ice cream as a dessert.*

Makes approximately 4 cups

Ingredients

2 mangos
6 oranges
1 tablespoon sherry
1 teaspoon lemon zest
½ teaspoon lime zest
1 vanilla bean, seeds removed and reserved
Pinch of nutmeg
3 tablespoons slivered almonds

Shopping List

Mangos
Oranges
Sherry
Lemon
Lime
Vanilla bean
Nutmeg
Slivered almonds

Tools and Equipment: Cutting board, knife, serving bowl, zester

Method

1.   Peel the mangos and remove the center seed. Cut the flesh into odd-shaped sizes, small enough to eat but not so small that they will get mushy when tossed. Put them in a large mixing bowl that is also suitable for serving in.

2.   Peel the oranges and remove their pith. Cut the oranges into odd-shaped sizes similar to the mango. Add them to the mangos.

3.   Add the sherry and stir well to coat the fruit. Let sit for about 10 minutes.

4.   Add the lemon and lime zests, vanilla seeds, and nutmeg, and toss to combine. Sprinkle with almonds.

Angela's Tips:
*To remove the vanilla seeds, slice the
bean open and scrape the seeds out.
Toasting almonds brings out their flavor
and you can opt to toast them before
adding to the salad.*

Orange and Strawberry Juice

*Try this fruit beverage for a nice change from straight orange juice.
It looks lovely in the glass when it's garnished with fresh fruit.
Add a little sparkle with a splash of club soda. Freeze some
strawberries overnight and pop them in the drink just before
serving for some edible ice cubes that won't dilute your drink.*

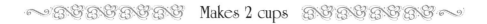

Makes 2 cups

Ingredients

12 strawberries
6 oranges, plus 2 for garnish
½ teaspoon vanilla extract or seeds scraped
   from ⅓ vanilla bean
Ice cubes

Shopping List

Strawberries
Oranges
Vanilla extract or vanilla
   bean

Tools and Equipment: Blender, knife, cutting board, citrus reamer or
manual juicer, mesh strainer

Method

1.   Remove the leaves from the strawberries. Put the strawberries in the blender and coarsely chop them.

2.   Cut the 6 oranges in half and juice them, using a citrus reamer or manual juicer. Add the juice to the strawberries then add the vanilla (or vanilla seeds). Blend until smooth.

3.   Cut the remaining oranges into slices about ¼ inch thick and put them in a pitcher along with the ice cubes.

4.   Pour the juice through a mesh strainer to remove the seeds and pulp then pour the strained juice over the ice and orange slices. Serve immediately.

Croissants
with
Strawberries, Mascarpone and Almonds

*Mascarpone cheese gets just the right sweetness from the
bit of sugar. Icing sugar maintains the soft texture of
the mascarpone—it's not as gritty as granulated sugar.
In the summer months when strawberries are at their most
luscious, you may need less sugar or even none at all!*

 Serves 4

Ingredients

10 to 12 strawberries
4 store-bought butter croissants
½ cup mascarpone cheese (2 tablespoons per
   croissant)
1 tablespoon icing sugar
1 teaspoon vanilla extract
½ vanilla bean and/or ½ teaspoon vanilla
   extract
⅓ cup slivered almonds

Shopping List

Strawberries
Butter croissants
Mascarpone cheese
Icing sugar
Vanilla extract
Vanilla bean (optional)
Slivered almond slices

Tools and Equipment: Knives (one to cut the croissants and strawberries
and one to spread the cheese), cutting board, toaster oven, mixing bowl,
wooden spoon

Method

1. Wash and dry the strawberries and remove their green tops. Thinly slice them lengthwise. Set aside until needed.

2. Split open each croissant lengthwise and lightly toast them in the toaster oven.

3. Mix together the mascarpone cheese, icing sugar, and vanilla extract.

4. Cut the vanilla bean in half lengthwise and scrape out the seeds from both sides with the tip of a spoon. Add the seeds to the cheese mixture to enhance the flavor and to make the cheese easier to spread.

5. Spread the toasted croissants with the cheese mixture.

6. On the bottom slice, top the cheese mixture with strawberries, sprinkle with almonds, and place the other croissant half on top.

Angela's Tip:
I like to use the extract and the seeds from the bean
together for a more aromatic vanilla flavor.

Smoked Salmon, Summer Fruits, Mascarpone Cheese and Croissant Plate

This is an easy-assembly dish. Add as much as you need for each guest, with more or less of a particular fruit according to taste, or include other fruits, such as seedless grapes or papaya. Serving the ingredients on an attractive platter somehow makes them taste even more delicious.

 Serves 4

Ingredients

Smoked salmon, 4 to 6 slices per person
Cantaloupe (½ serves 4)
Strawberries, 3 to 4 per person
Bananas, ⅓ per person
Kiwis, ½ per person
Mascarpone cheese (1 cup serves 4)
Vanilla extract (1 teaspoon per cup of mascarpone)
Icing sugar (2 teaspoons per cup of mascarpone)
Lemon zest (1 teaspoon per cup of mascarpone)
Croissants

Shopping List

Smoked salmon
Cantaloupe
Strawberries
Bananas
Kiwis
Mascarpone cheese
Vanilla extract
Icing sugar
Lemon zest
Croissants

Tools and Equipment: Knife, cutting board, vegetable peeler, platter, mixing bowl, spoon

Method

1.   Roll the slices of smoked salmon into loose rolls.

2.   Cut the cantaloupe in half, scoop out the seeds, and peel and slice each half into 4 pieces. Arrange them on the platter, fanning them along its edge.

3.   Make fanned strawberries (see instructions below).

4.   Peel the bananas and cut them into diagonal slices. Arrange the slices in an overlapping pattern beside the cantaloupe.

5.   Peel the kiwis and slice them. Arrange the slices in an overlapping pattern beside the banana slices.

6.   Mix the mascarpone cheese with the vanilla extract, icing sugar, and lemon zest.

7.   Place a dollop of cheese on the platter for guests to spread on croissants and to dip fruit into on their own plates. Croissants can be served as you like them: either room temperature or warmed, and sliced and toasted or in a basket beside the platter.

Fanning a Strawberry
Using a paring knife, slice the strawberry from a point just slightly below the top stem to the bottom. Continue making these slits from one end of the strawberry to the other. Gently spread the strawberry apart to create the fan shape.

Parisian Breakfast

Sometimes, when I'm in the mood, I have this simple breakfast on my front step where a bistro table and chairs sit ready for special moments. A lacy wisteria creeps down and into the space overhead, and in the summer mornings the light is just right, soft and warm. On a Sunday morning, it's quiet, with only the chirping of the birds, and the scent of flowers hangs in the air. This is when I take this breakfast to sit at the bistro table, greet the morning, and look out over the garden.

 Serves 2

Ingredients

2 cafés au lait (ingredients: espresso, hot milk, and sugar if desired)
2 pains au chocolat (chocolate croissants)
Whole strawberries
Cantaloupe slices

Shopping List

Espresso roast coffee
Milk
Pains au chocolat
Sugar (optional)
Strawberries
Cantaloupe

Tools and Equipment: To make this a beautiful breakfast, break out your finest tableware and cups and saucers to enjoy this lovely indulgent breakfast. You'll also need a sharp knife for slicing the fruit

Method

This is a simple-assembly breakfast with no real recipe. The presentation is important, so pay attention to detail. Use your best china and a pretty serving tray.

1.   Make the espresso. Heat an equal amount of milk in the microwave. While the coffee is steeping in the French press or being made on the stove, assemble the plates and the pains au chocolat on a pretty tray. Make a strawberry fan garnish (see page 33).

2.   Slice the cantaloupe and arrange the slices in a pleasing presentation. Fanned-out slices are especially attractive.

3.   Prepare the café au lait and serve in bowls.

Angela's Tip:
Look for chocolate croissants in the bakery section of your supermarket, your local bakery, or anywhere baked goods are sold.

What Is Café au Lait?
Café au lait is similar to latte. By definition, it is milky strong coffee traditionally made with a strong coffee such as espresso. Espresso is not defined by the machine it is made in, but is a roasting type. My favorite—and the easiest—method for making any coffee is to use an espresso roast in a French press rather than on the stove. It adds a lovely flavor to a café au lait. In France, this coffee is usually drunk only in the morning, from large bowls with no handles. I always feel like a little kitten drinking this milky coffee out of the bowl.

Lunch or Light Dinner

About lunch

Lunch, the abbreviation of luncheon, which means a light midday meal, now refers to any meal served at midday. It was referred to as dinner in the 18th century and was consumed between two and four in the afternoon, which is typically when Christmas and Thanksgiving meals are served. In London during the 1730s and 1740s, the upper class dined around three or four in the afternoon, but by 1770, the time for dinner had moved to around four or five. Typically these meals were served by candlelight and were a formal meal sometimes with entertainment, known in Regency times as the "supper party."

Here are some gourmet twists on lunch.

Enjoy!

Chicken and Brie Sandwiches
with
Balsamic Onions

*The great flavors and textures in this sandwich have made it
a favorite at my cooking demonstrations, as well as at home.
Serve it with a beverage for a simple lunch or with a salad
for a light dinner. In a pinch, use a rotisserie chicken from the
supermarket rather than cooking the chicken breast beforehand.
Toasting the bread gives a little extra flavor and crunch.*

 Makes 2 sandwiches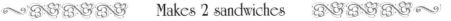

Ingredients

4 thick slices bakery bread
2 teaspoons mayonnaise (one per sandwich)
2 teaspoons fig or apricot jam
Sliced cooked chicken breast
Brie cheese (3 to 4 slices per sandwich)
2 tablespoons balsamic onions (one per
    sandwich) (see recipe on page 66)
One ripe pear, unpeeled, cored, and thinly
    sliced
4 leaves butter lettuce (2 leaves per
    sandwich)

Shopping List

Bakery bread, thick sliced
Mayonnaise
Fig or apricot jam
Chicken breast
Brie cheese
Pear
Butter lettuce

Tools and Equipment: Knife for spreading, measuring spoon, melon
baller (for coring the pear), knife for cutting, cutting board

Method

SEE PAGE 66 FOR BALSAMIC ONION RECIPE.

1.   Arrange the slices of bread on the work surface.

2.   Spread the mayo lightly on one slice and the jam on the other.

3.   Place the chicken slices on the mayo side of each pair, covering the bread. Top with the Brie slices.

4.   Spread out the balsamic onions over the layer of Brie. Top with pear slices. Add two leaves of butter lettuce per sandwich.

5.   Put the jam-covered bread slice on the sandwich, jam side down. Slice into two triangles.

Simple Salad

I love salads, especially ones containing a lot of different ingredients like fruits and nuts. Not only do they provide extra nutrition they also make the salad more exciting to the palate. You can create some great tastes by using different fruit and cheese combinations with the baby greens: blueberries and mozzarella, goat cheese and strawberries, or grapefruit and spinach. Add what you like—use more fruit, fewer vegetables, whatever you're in the mood for. Let your imagination run wild!

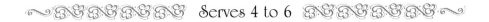

Serves 4 to 6

Ingredients

6 cups mixed baby greens
3 Roma tomatoes
½ English cucumber
3 tablespoons pine nuts
½ cup green olives, pitted
¼ teaspoon sea salt
1½ tablespoons olive oil
1 teaspoon red wine vinegar
¼ cup crumbled goat cheese

Shopping List

Mixed baby greens
Roma tomatoes
English cucumber
Pine nuts
Green olives
Sea salt
Olive oil
Red wine vinegar
Goat cheese

Tools and Equipment: Salad bowl, knife, cutting board, wooden spoons for tossing

Method

1. Put the salad greens in a large bowl that can be used as a serving bowl.

2. Thinly slice the tomatoes and cucumber. Add them to the salad greens. Add the pine nuts, olives, and sea salt. Toss the ingredients together.

3. Add the olive oil, gently toss, then add the vinegar and toss. Add the goat cheese and gently toss to combine. Serve.

Smoked Salmon, Brie and Balsamic Portobello Mushroom Baguette

A baguette is the perfect bread for these summery sandwiches.
Cut the baguette into whatever size is appropriate for your needs.

 Makes 4 sandwiches

Ingredients

2 large Portobello mushrooms, stems removed
2 tablespoons olive oil
¼ cup balsamic vinegar
½ teaspoon sea salt
Fresh bakery baguette
4 tablespoons mayonnaise, mixed with
   1 teaspoon of dill
Smoked salmon (2 to 3 slices per sandwich)
Brie (2 slices per sandwich)
Butter lettuce leaves
Pepper, black, to taste

Shopping List

Portobello mushrooms
Olive oil
Balsamic vinegar
Sea salt
Fresh bakery baguette
Mayonnaise
Dill
Smoked salmon
Brie
Butter lettuce
Pepper, black

Tools and Equipment: Toaster oven, aluminum foil, knife, cutting board, medium-sized bowl, knife for spreading

Method

FOR THE BALSAMIC PORTOBELLO MUSHROOMS: *MAKE AHEAD*

Line the toaster oven tray with aluminum foil. Preheat the toaster oven to 375 degrees F.

1.   Cut the mushrooms in ½-inch slices. Put them in a medium-sized bowl and toss with the olive oil until well coated. Add the balsamic vinegar and salt, and toss until well coated.

2.   Arrange the slices in a single layer (slightly overlapping is fine) and bake in the toaster oven until soft, about 10 to 15 minutes.

ASSEMBLE THE SANDWICH:

1.   Cut the baguette into four equal pieces, and slice each piece in half horizontally. Toast the pieces lightly then lay them out on a clean work surface. Spread the mayonnaise on the top and bottom pieces of bread. Lay the salmon pieces on the bottom half and top with the mushrooms, then the Brie and butter lettuce. Add pepper to taste. Put the top half in place and cut in half on a diagonal. Serve.

43

Fancy Tuna Melt
with
Fine Herbs Mayonnaise and Swiss Cheese

This is comfort food with a little gourmet twist.
It makes a light evening meal with a simple summer
salad, or a substantial lunch on its own.

 Makes 2

Ingredients

2 slices bread
1 can tuna
¼ teaspoon fresh lemon juice
2 tablespoons mayonnaise
1 teaspoon dried tarragon
1 teaspoon fresh chives
¼ teaspoon sea salt
Pepper, black, to taste
2 slices Swiss cheese

Shopping List

Bread
Canned tuna
Lemon juice
Mayonnaise
Dried tarragon
Fresh chives
Sea salt
Pepper, black
Swiss cheese

Tools and Equipment: Can opener, medium-sized bowl, spoon, spreading knife

Method

Line the toaster oven tray with a piece of aluminum foil. Preheat the toaster oven to 350 degrees F.

1.   Lay out the slices of bread on the work surface.

2.   Drain the canned tuna gently so it is still slightly moist. Put the tuna in a medium-sized mixing bowl then add the lemon juice, mayonnaise, tarragon, chives, salt, and pepper. Mix until well combined.

3.   Evenly distribute the tuna onto the two slices of bread and top each with a slice of Swiss cheese.

4.   Heat them in the toaster oven until the cheese is melted. Serve.

Simple Summer Salad with Fruit

This is the time of year for salads.
Using a variety of fresh ingredients can turn this salad into a
delicious addition to a meal or make it a little meal in itself.

Serves 2 as a light meal, 4 as a side

Ingredients

2 cups butter lettuce
2 cups spinach leaves
8 strawberries
1 orange
½ cup mango or cantaloupe
⅛ teaspoon sea salt
½ tablespoons white wine vinegar
  or pear vinegar
2 tablespoons olive oil
¼ cup blueberries
1 tablespoon (or more to taste) crushed
  pistachios for garnish

Shopping List

Butter lettuce
Spinach leaves
Strawberries
Oranges
Mango or cantaloupe
Sea salt
White wine vinegar or
  pear vinegar
Olive oil
Blueberries

Tools and Equipment: Cutting board, knife, salad bowl, 2 spoons for tossing salad

Method

1.   Wash and dry the lettuce and spinach. Tear up the lettuce and place it in a mixing bowl. Hull and slice the strawberries lengthwise. Peel and remove the pith of the oranges and cut into chunks. Add these to the salad.

2.   Cut the mango or cantaloupe into odd-shaped chunks. They do not have to be even. This salad looks better with a more rustic look and not so finely or perfectly chopped fruits. Add into the salad.

3.   After each item is added, toss the salad, starting with sea salt, then vinegar and finish with the olive oil.

4.   Top with the blueberries and chopped pistachios.

Dinner

About dinner

Traditionally, dinner was primarily the largest meal of the day for those who lived in suburbia and worked in non-agricultural jobs. It was eaten between noon and 1 pm mainly because artificial lighting was expensive and inefficient, so people ended the day and went to bed at sundown. Times sure have changed. We can now eat anytime of the day regardless of the darkness.

Summer is typically a time for lighter meals, but you still need something substantial and satisfying. These pleasant seasonal meals need not be complicated and may be assembled simply by adding more quantity or an added salad with a few extra ingredients like cooked potatoes or fruit. The addition of another vegetable dish can also be very satisfying while not being overly filling, still leaving plenty of room for dessert!

Here are some of my family's favorite summer meals.

Enjoy!

Gourmet Dinner Salad
with
Rotisserie Chicken or Smoked Salmon

Looking for a quick yet tasty dinner for tonight? Stop at the supermarket on your way home and pick up a rotisserie chicken for this gourmet take on fast food. There is relatively little oil in this recipe as the salad can get soggy if you overdo it. However, if the greens seem too dry, you can always add more according to taste.

 Serves 6

Ingredients

5 cups salad greens
1 store-bought rotisserie chicken, shredded
1 pear
½ cucumber, English
½ bulb fennel
3 Belgian endives
1 jar (170 ml) artichoke hearts packed in oil, drained
2 tomatoes, cut into 8 slices each
¼ teaspoon sea salt
1 tablespoon olive oil
2 teaspoons red wine vinegar
½ cup dried cherries or cranberries
¼ cup goat cheese, crumbled

Shopping List

Salad greens
Rotisserie chicken
Pear
Cucumber
Fennel bulb
Belgian endives
Jar of artichoke hearts packed in oil
Tomatoes
Sea salt
Olive oil
Red wine vinegar
Dried cherries or cranberries
Goat cheese

Tools and Equipment: Large salad bowl, food processor, large spoons for tossing salad

Method

1. Wash and dry the salad greens. Put the greens in a large salad bowl. Add the chicken.

2. In a food processor, thinly slice the pear, cucumber, fennel, and Belgian endives. Toss with the greens.

3. Add the drained artichokes (leave a little oil on them to go into the salad) and tomato slices.

4. Add the salt and toss. Add the olive oil and toss again.

5. Add the red wine vinegar and toss again.

6. Add the cherries and goat cheese. Toss and serve.

Angela's Tip
This is another salad you can have fun with by making substitutions. Add or substitute any of the following: green beans, cooked potatoes, carrots, crisp fruits such as apples. Vary the lettuces as well or combine several kinds. The only lettuce that doesn't work well is iceberg lettuce.

Pasta
with
Zucchini, Artichokes and Capers
with
Parmesan

I love the ribbons of vegetables in this dish. Not only do they appeal to your visual sense, but your taste buds will appreciate them too. This preparation method is one of the fastest for cooking vegetables, and fast means more nutrients are retained after cooking. Using the toaster oven and the microwave keeps the temperature down in the kitchen. Even the pasta is cooked in the microwave!

 Serves 6

Ingredients

½ red onion
Sea salt
3 teaspoons olive oil
1 zucchini
½ pound fresh pasta (any style, without fillings)
1 jar (13 ounce) artichokes in olive oil
2 tablespoons capers
⅓ cup grated or shaved Parmesan cheese
Pepper to taste, black or mixed

Shopping List

Red onion
Sea salt
Olive oil
Zucchini
Fresh pasta, such as fettuccini or other pastas without fillings
Artichokes in olive oil
Capers
Parmesan cheese
Pepper, black or mixed

Tools and Equipment: Toaster oven, aluminum foil, knife, cutting board, vegetable peeler, microwave-safe pot for cooking pasta, microwave, wooden spoon, grater or vegetable peeler to shave the Parmesan cheese

Method

FOR THE ONION:

Line the toaster oven tray with aluminum foil. Preheat the toaster oven to 375 degrees F.

1.   Peel and slice the onion. Sprinkle a pinch of sea salt on the slices and toss to distribute. Drizzle over about 1 teaspoon of olive oil and toss to coat evenly.

2.   Lay the onion slices on the aluminum foil and cook them in the toaster oven until translucent, about 10 minutes.

3.   Take out and set aside.

FOR THE ZUCCHINI:

Line the toaster oven tray with aluminum foil. Preheat the toaster oven to 375 degrees F.

1   Peel the zucchini. Continue to use the peeler to create long ribbons of zucchini flesh. Sprinkle a pinch of sea salt on the ribbons and toss to distribute evenly. Drizzle over about 2 teaspoons of olive oil and toss.

2.   Lay the zucchini slices on the aluminum foil and cook in the toaster oven for about 10 minutes or until they pierce easily with a knife.

3.   Take out and set aside.

FOR THE PASTA:

1.   Pour about 3 cups of water into a 1½-quart microwave-safe deep pot. Heat for 2½ to 3 minutes at 100% power until the water boils. Add 1 teaspoon salt to the water and stir.

2.   Spread out the pasta in the pot. Cook for 6 to 8 minutes at 50% power until the pasta is done to your liking. Drain off any remaining water.

ASSEMBLING THE PASTA:

1.   Drain the artichokes and blot them lightly. Put them into a large bowl along with the cooked pasta, onions, and vegetables. Toss to combine.

2.   Add the capers and Parmesan and toss. Add pepper to taste. Serve.

Mango Coconut Chicken

I made this dish one summer when I was looking for something exciting and light for a summer meal. It was a smash hit. And it came with a bonus—the leftovers were terrific in a sandwich the next day.

 Serves 4

Ingredients

4 cups torn or shredded cooked chicken
    (about 3 medium-size chicken breasts)
½ cup shredded sweetened coconut
1 tablespoon fresh lemon juice
1 tablespoon Dijon mustard
3 tablespoons Major Grey mango chutney
    (see Angela's Tip for more information)
½ cup plain yogurt
½ cup coarsely chopped Italian parsley
½ teaspoon sea salt
Pepper, black, to taste

Shopping List

Chicken
Sweetened shredded coconut
Lemon
Dijon mustard
Mango chutney—Major Grey
Plain yogurt
Italian parsley
Sea salt
Pepper, black

Tools and Equipment: Measuring cup and spoons, cutting board, knife, medium-size mixing bowl, wooden spoon

Method

1. Put the shredded chicken pieces into a medium-size bowl.

2. Add the coconut, lemon juice, Dijon mustard, chutney, and yogurt and toss until well combined. Add the parsley and toss until combined. Stir in the salt and pepper. Serve.

Angela's Tip:
Major Grey is not a brand of chutney, it is a style of chutney. Look for it under various brand names in your supermarket in the condiment or ethnic section.

Chicken
with
Dijon Vinaigrette, Fennel and Apples,
with
Thyme Potatoes

Apple and fennel are such a great combination in their textures and flavors. This dish gets even easier to prepare if you make the potatoes and cook the fennel and apple ahead of time.

Serves 4 to 6

Ingredients

1 bulb fennel
1 Granny Smith apple, halved and cored
1 pound potatoes
1 tablespoon butter
1 teaspoon sea salt
Pepper, black, to taste
2 to 3 sprigs fresh thyme
2 tablespoons Dijon mustard
1 tablespoon white wine vinegar
1 tablespoon sherry
½ cup olive oil
1 store-bought rotisserie chicken, shredded
⅓ cup chopped Italian parsley

Shopping List

Fennel
Granny Smith apple
Potatoes
Fresh thyme
Butter
Sea salt
Pepper, black
Dijon mustard
White wine vinegar
Sherry
Olive oil
Rotisserie chicken
Italian parsley

Tools and Equipment: Knife, cutting board, microwave-safe dish, microwave-safe silicone cover, whisk, small mixing bowl, large serving bowl, measuring spoons

Method

1.   Cut the fennel core out and slice the remaining fennel into ¼-inch slices. Cut the apple into cubes. Put the fennel and apple in a microwave-safe dish and cover with a silicone microwave-safe lid. Cook for about 4 minutes on 100% power, or until the apple can be pierced easily with a knife.

2.   Being careful of the steam, remove the dish lid and drain any water. Set aside the apple and fennel until needed.

3.   Wash the potatoes. Cut them up and put them in a microwave-safe dish, covered with a microwave-safe silicone lid. Cook for about 10 minutes or until they pierce easily with a knife. Being careful of the steam, remove the lid. Add the butter, sea salt, pepper, and thyme and toss. Set aside until needed.

4.   Put the Dijon mustard, a pinch of sea salt, vinegar, and sherry in a small bowl. Whisk them together and slowly pour in the olive oil, whisking to form an emulsion (see Angela's Tip below).

5.   In a large serving bowl, combine the chicken, apple, fennel, potatoes, Dijon vinaigrette, and chopped parsley. Toss to combine.

Angela's Tip:
Because oil and vinegar do not mix, you need an emulsifier like mayonnaise or mustard to make the ingredients combine well. Without an emulsifier, the vinaigrette will soon separate.

Asparagus Spears Wrapped with Prosciutto
with
Herbed Risotto
and
Mixed Baby Greens with Mandarin and Pistachios

Put the rice on to cook while you prepare the other parts of the recipe for a perfectly timed meal. A fast and elegant meal.

 Serves 4

Ingredients

1 cup arborio rice (risotto)
2½ cups warm chicken stock
1½ teaspoon sea salt
1 tablespoon butter
1 teaspoon dried tarragon
1 teaspoon dried chives
1 teaspoon chopped Italian parsley
12 asparagus spears
2 teaspoons olive oil
4 slices prosciutto
½ cup pistachios, salted and crushed
8 cups mixed baby greens
1 can (11 ounce) mandarin oranges, drained
3 teaspoons red wine vinegar
4 teaspoons Dijon mustard

Shopping List

Arborio rice (risotto)
Chicken stock
Sea salt
Butter
Dried tarragon
Dried chives
Italian parsley
Asparagus spears
Olive oil
Prosciutto slices
Shelled pistachios
Mixed baby greens
Mandarin oranges
Red wine vinegar
Dijon mustard

Tools and Equipment: Knife, cutting board, microwave-safe bowl, measuring cup, measuring spoon, aluminum foil, mixing spoons

Method

Line the toaster oven tray with aluminum foil. Preheat the toaster oven to 400 degrees F.

1.   Put the rice and chicken stock in a microwave-safe bowl. Cover with a silicone cover and cook for 20 minutes at 100% power, stirring halfway through. Once the rice is cooked, take it out of the oven and uncover it immediately, being careful of the steam. Add 1 teaspoon of the salt, all the butter, the tarragon, the chives, and the parsley and toss to combine. Set aside until needed.

2.   While the risotto is cooking, wash and trim the asparagus spears. Lay the spears on the toaster oven tray. Drizzle with 1 teaspoon of the olive oil and sprinkle evenly with the remaining ½ teaspoon of sea salt. Roast the spears in the toaster oven for 10 to 12 minutes or until they can be pierced easily with a knife. The asparagus should be cooked but still a bit firm. Remove from the oven and let cool.

3.   Wrap a slice of prosciutto around the bottom of three asparagus spears and set aside. Repeat with the remaining spears.

4.   Lightly toast the pistachios on a foil-lined toaster oven tray, using clean foil, until they are lightly browned and smell nutty, 7 to 10 minutes.

5.   In a large bowl, mix the baby greens, mandarin oranges, and pistachios. Toss first with the remaining sea salt, and then the remaining olive oil, and toss again. Add the vinegar and toss well.

6.   Place one trio of prosciutto spears on each plate and serve alongside the serving of risotto.

7.   Add a serving of the salad to each plate and 1 teaspoon of Dijon mustard for each serving.

Bean Salad
with
White Balsamic Vinaigrette

A quintessential summer dish contains herbs.
Fresh and light, this simple combination of everyday
ingredients transforms into a bowl full of summer flavor.

 Makes 4½ to 5 cups

Ingredients

1 can (16 ounce) chickpeas (about 1½ cups)
1 can (16 ounce) white beans (about 1½ cups)
1 can (16 ounce) kidney beans (about 1½ cups)
2 teaspoons minced garlic
1 teaspoon sea salt, or more to taste
⅓ cup chopped Italian parsley
2 teaspoons chopped fresh chives
1 teaspoon dried tarragon
1½ tablespoons olive oil
1½ tablespoons Dijon mustard
1 tablespoon white balsamic vinegar
Pepper, black, to taste

Shopping List

Chickpeas
White beans
Kidney beans
Garlic
Sea salt
Italian parsley
Fresh chives
Dried tarragon
Olive oil
Dijon mustard
White balsamic vinegar
Pepper, black

Tools and Equipment: Bowl, strainer, knife, cutting board, measuring spoons, mixing spoons

Method

1.   Drain the chickpeas and beans and put them in a large mixing bowl. Add the garlic and salt, and toss to combine. Add the parsley, chives, and tarragon and toss again.

2.   Add the olive oil and mustard, and toss until coated. Add the balsamic vinegar and toss. Just before serving, add a dusting of pepper.

Ham and Parmesan Sandwiches
with
Herbed Mayonnaise and Apricot Jam

*The extra detail of the herbs in the mayonnaise and apricot
jam really gives a simple ham sandwich something special.
Note that butter lettuce is also known as Boston or Bibb lettuce.*

 Serves 4

Ingredients

8 slices fresh bakery bread, unsliced or sliced
   thick at the bakery
1 teaspoon finely chopped fresh rosemary
1 teaspoon finely chopped fresh Italian parsley
3 tablespoons mayonnaise
Pepper, black, to taste
2 tablespoons apricot jam
Roasted Black Forest or peppered ham, thickly
   sliced, enough for 4 sandwiches
2 teaspoons Dijon mustard (½ teaspoon per
   sandwich)
Parmesan cheese, sliced with vegetable peeler
   into thin slices
Butter lettuce, 2 leaves per sandwich

Shopping List

Fresh bakery bread
Fresh rosemary
Italian parsley
Mayonnaise
Pepper, black
Apricot jam
Ham roast
Dijon mustard
Fresh Parmesan cheese
Butter lettuce

Tools and Equipment: Knife, cutting board, measuring spoon, small
mixing bowl, vegetable peeler

Method

1. Slice the bread to the desired thickness or have the bakery cut the loaf in large slices (Texas-toast sized). Lay the slices out on the work surface.

2. In a small bowl, mix the rosemary and parsley with the mayonnaise and stir until combined.

3. Spread the mayonnaise on one slice of each sandwich and sprinkle with pepper. Spread the apricot jam on the other slices. Put the cooked ham on the mayonnaise side and top with mustard.

4. Put the Parmesan cheese slices on the ham slices.

5. Top with the lettuce leaves. Put the slices with the jam on top of the other slices. Cut in half.

Toaster Oven Roasted Balsamic Tomatoes

One summer my husband came home with a whole flat of cherry tomatoes. Beautiful, plump, and juicy, from a client of his who owned a greenhouse. I looked at them and knew I wanted to make sure none of them went to waste. Wasting food makes me sad! So, I decided to roast them and store them in jars. We sent a jar back to the greenhouse people and they loved them!

 Makes 1 cup

Ingredients

1½ cups cherry tomatoes
3 tablespoons balsamic vinegar
½ tablespoon olive oil
¼ teaspoon sugar (if the tomatoes are really ripe, skip the sugar)
½ teaspoon sea salt
Pepper, black, ground, to taste

Shopping List

Cherry tomatoes
Balsamic vinegar
Olive oil
Sugar
Sea salt
Ground pepper, black

Tools and Equipment: Toaster oven and tray, aluminum foil, knife, cutting board

Method

Line the toaster oven tray with aluminum foil. Preheat the toaster oven to 375 degrees F.

1.   Wash and cut the tomatoes in half and toss with the vinegar, olive oil, sugar, and sea salt.

2.   Spread onto the toaster oven tray and roast until they pierce easily with a knife, about 20 minutes.

Balsamic Onions

*I rely on these sweet, caramel onions as a secret ingredient and staple
condiment. I use them wherever onions are called for in a recipe.
The soft, delicious texture of the balsamic onions gives any dish
instant depth and a complex flavor. They will add an extra flavor
to meat or poultry dishes and they're terrific served on the side
with scrambled eggs. On a practical level, you save time by making
up a batch of these as you won't have to take extra time to
cook onions every time they are needed. I always make more than
I need as they will keep in the fridge for months.*

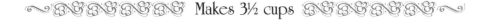

Makes 3½ cups

Ingredients

4 large onions
1 tablespoon margarine
4 tablespoons balsamic vinegar
2 teaspoons sugar
¼ teaspoon sea salt

Shopping List

Large onions
Margarine
Balsamic vinegar
Sugar
Sea salt

Tools and Equipment: Large saucepan, stirrer, knife, cutting board

Method —requires a stove

MAKE AHEAD

1.   Peel the onions and slice them in half from top to bottom. Trim the top and bottom of each half.

2.   Cut the onion halves into chunks by cutting at right angles to the original cut. Make the pieces as consistently sized as possible so they will cook evenly. A medium-sized onion can be cut into pieces of about ¼ inch.

3.   Set a large saucepan on the stove over medium-high heat and let it warm up. Add the margarine to the pan. When the margarine melts and begins to bubble, add the onions. Stir the onions so that they are well coated. Cook for about 5 minutes or until the onions begin to sweat (look glossy).

4.   Add the balsamic vinegar, sugar, and salt.

5.   Continue cooking on low heat for about 15 to 20 minutes until the onions have softened, stirring occasionally.

6.   Take the pan off the heat and serve warm. If making ahead, allow the onions to cool and then store them in an airtight container in the fridge.

Dessert

About dessert

Just about everybody loves desserts! In Europe desserts have been a gastronomic obsession for centuries. They are always good, anytime, in my opinion. I even love to start the day with a dessert-type of breakfast, topped off with a cup of coffee.

Desserts need not be overly sweet to be enjoyable. Some of my favorites are fruit desserts and these are also some of the more simple ones to prepare.

Here are some of my favorite summer desserts.

Enjoy!

Summer Mangos with Nutmeg

This recipe came about by happy accident. It was another time when my husband came home with an abundance of produce—this time it was a flat of mangos. They were ripe and ready for eating. I couldn't imagine how we could use so many mangos before they went off. Following my nose to the spice cabinet, I came up with this succulent dish.

 Makes approximately 1½ cups

Ingredients

1 ripe mango, peeled and cut into large pieces
2 teaspoons butter
2 teaspoons brown sugar
Pinch of nutmeg

Shopping List

Mango
Butter
Brown sugar
Nutmeg

Tools and Equipment: Knife, cutting board, ovenproof dish

Method

Preheat the toaster oven to 350 degrees F.

1.   Put the cut mango pieces into a small ovenproof dish.

2.   Dot the mango pieces with the butter and sprinkle them evenly with the brown sugar and nutmeg.

3.   Cook for 10 minutes for succulent mangos, or 20 minutes for a more intense flavor.

4.   Coat each mango piece with the glossy, sugary juices in the dish. Serve alone, with ice cream, or on the side of your favorite dessert.

Apples with Vanilla and Lavender

The delicate flavor of lavender flowers gives this dish a surprising and delightful taste. This was a huge hit at the first No-Cook Cooking demonstration I gave. If you have trouble finding lavender flowers, try a tea merchant or specialty tea shop. You'll also find suppliers on the Internet.

 Makes 2 cups

Ingredients

3 to 4 apples, depending on the size (Royal Gala, Empire, Fuji or other baking apples)
1½ teaspoons vanilla extract
2 tablespoons brown sugar
1 teaspoon sherry
1 teaspoon cinnamon
Nutmeg
1 teaspoon lavender flowers

Shopping List

Apples, 3 to 4 depending on the size (Royal Gala, Empire, Fuji, or other baking apples)
Vanilla extract
Brown sugar
Sherry
Cinnamon
Nutmeg
Lavender flowers

Tools and Equipment: Pastry brush, shallow microwave-safe dish, vegetable peeler, knife, cutting board, measuring spoon

Method

Lightly butter shallow microwave-safe dish.

1.   Peel the apples, cut them in half, then core them and slice them into 6 to 8 slices. Spread them out over the bottom of the buttered baking dish. Sprinkle with the vanilla, sugar, sherry, cinnamon, a pinch of nutmeg, and half the lavender flowers. Cook at 100% power for about 7 minutes or until the apples are softened and pierce easily with a knife.

2.   Transfer the apples to a serving dish and sprinkle with the remaining lavender flowers.

Angela's Tip:
Don't have a pastry brush for buttering the dish? Use a piece of parchment paper to spread the butter.

Cold Melon Soup with Port

Here's a refreshing soup to serve between courses or as a dessert. If it sits for a little while, stir it before serving. Be prepared for guests to ask for seconds! You can make a non-alcoholic version by replacing the port with pomegranate juice.

 Makes approximately 5 cups

Ingredients

1 cantaloupe
½ honeydew melon
⅓ cup orange juice
6 strawberries or cherries
3 tablespoons port
2 tablespoons honey (or more to taste)
1 teaspoon vanilla extract
Mint leaves for garnish

Shopping List

Cantaloupe
Honeydew melon
Orange juice
Strawberries or cherries
Port
Honey
Vanilla extract
Mint leaves

Tools and Equipment: Knife, cutting board, peeler, blender, measuring cup, measuring spoon

Method

1.   Peel the cantaloupe and honeydew melon and cut them into small chunks. Put them in a blender.

2.   Add the orange juice and blend until smooth.

3.   Add the berries, port, honey, and vanilla. Purée.

4.   Serve in shallow bowls garnished with mint leaves and a few berries if you have extra, or toast cubes of angel food cake lightly in the toaster oven and sprinkle on top like sweet little croutons.

Strawberries and Cream Soup

*This is such a refreshing and summery soup with a flavor that
I equate with summer. Nothing beats strawberries and cream.
Use fresh strawberries when in season from your local farmers.
Nothing beats their taste!*

 Makes 4½ to 5 cups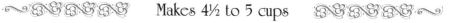

Ingredients

3 pints strawberries, washed and hulled
1 cup icing sugar
1 pint half-and-half or whole milk
¾ cup vanilla yogurt
⅛ teaspoon lemon zest
1 teaspoon vanilla extract
1 tablespoon sherry
Pinch of nutmeg

Shopping List

Strawberries, washed
   and hulled
Icing sugar
Half-and-half or whole
   milk
Vanilla yogurt
Lemon zest
Vanilla extract
Sherry
Nutmeg

Tools and Equipment: Knife, cutting board, blender, measuring cup,
measuring spoon

Method

1. Keep 6 strawberries aside for a garnish. Purée the remaining strawberries with the icing sugar in a blender.

2. Strain through a sieve to remove the seeds and set aside.

3. Whisk the half-and-half, yogurt, lemon zest, vanilla, sherry, and nutmeg together until well blended.

4. Fold in the strawberry mixture and chill. Thinly slice the reserved strawberries.

5. Pour the soup into individual bowls and serve with two slices of strawberry on top.

Blueberry Lemon Pie with Custard

Lemon is a refreshing summertime flavor and sets off
another tasty summertime treat—fresh blueberries—in this
easy-to-make dessert. You'll save time and energy by
using a ready-made pie crust and canned custard.
Note: You will need a toaster oven that holds a 9-inch pie plate.

 Serves 6

Ingredients

1 ready-made frozen pie crust
3 cups blueberries
3 tablespoons sugar
2 teaspoons sherry
1 tablespoon lemon zest
1½ cups canned Devon custard or other
   good-quality custard
1 tablespoon sliced almonds
Whipping cream (as much or as little as you
   want!)
Icing sugar (about 2 tablespoons per cup
   cream)
Vanilla extract (1 teaspoon per cup cream)

Shopping List

Frozen pie crust
Blueberries
Sugar
Sherry
Lemon
Canned custard
Sliced almonds
Whipping cream
Icing sugar
Vanilla extract

Tools and Equipment: Measuring cup, measuring spoons, mixing bowl,
zester, mixer (hand or stand)

Method

MAKE AHEAD

Preheat the toaster oven to 350 degrees F. Prick the pastry bottom with a fork so it can vent.

1.   In the toaster over, blind bake the pie crust (see Angela's Tip below) until it's lightly browned, 10 to 12 minutes. Let the pie crust cool after baking.

2.   Wash and drain the blueberries and put them in a mixing bowl. Add the sugar, sherry, and lemon zest and stir gently to coat the berries. Set aside.

3.   Spread the custard in the bottom of the cooled pie crust and top with the blueberry mixture. Sprinkle the almonds on top and refrigerate for 30 minutes or until you're ready to serve dessert.

4.   Whip the cream with icing sugar and vanilla. Serve a dollop with each slice of pie.

Angela's Tips:
When blind baking a pastry crust, keep the pastry from puffing up by setting pie weights, or dried beans or rice tied up in cheesecloth, on the bottom of the crust.
Use icing sugar to sweeten cream when whipping it. Icing sugar acts as a stabilizer becasue it contains some cornstarch. It also dissolves and does not have a crunchy texture.

Angel Food Cake
with
Fruit Compote and Custard

It does not get any simpler—or cooler—than this!
Cake and canned custard from the grocery store and a fruit
compote made in less than 10 minutes in the microwave.
Topped with whipped cream, it's simply delicious!

 Makes 4 servings

Ingredients

FOR THE COMPOTE

3 to 4 apples (Royal Gala, Empire, or Fuji)
1 teaspoon butter
2 teaspoons sugar
½ teaspoon cinnamon
1 teaspoon vanilla extract
1 tablespoon orange zest

FOR THE CAKE

1 store-bought angel food cake
1½ cups Devon-style canned custard
Whipping cream (optional)
4 strawberries

Shopping List

Apples (Royal Gala,
   Empire, or Fuji)
Butter
Sugar
Cinnamon
Vanilla extract
Orange zest
Angel food cake
Canned custard (a
   Devon-style custard
   is a great choice)
Whipping cream
   (optional)

Tools and Equipment: Microwave-safe dish, zester, knife, cutting board,
vegetable peeler, spoon, serving plates

Method

1.   Peel the apples then core them and cut them up. Place in a microwave-safe dish for cooking. Add the butter, sugar, cinnamon, vanilla extract, and orange zest. Toss to combine. Cover with a microwave-safe silicone cover and microwave until the apples pierce easily with a knife, about 7 minutes.

2.   Take out of the microwave, uncover, and set aside until needed.

ASSEMBLING THE DESSERT:

1.   Cut up the cake to make four 3-inch wide slices. Place one on each plate.

2.   Spoon custard over half the cake, allowing it to pool around the corner and side.

3.   Spoon apple compote in a small heap at the base of the cake in the pool of custard. Top with whipped cream, if using, and garnish with a strawberry fan (see page 33). Serve.

Lavender Brownies with Cherries

A chic take on a brownie. These make a decadent dessert when served with whipped cream or ice cream, or just serve them by themselves with your favorite beverage. Either way, they are just delicious! Note: You will need a toaster oven that holds an 8-inch by 8-inch pan. Otherwise, divide the batter between two smaller dishes and bake each separately. The cooking time remains the same.

 Makes one 8-inch by 8-inch pan

Ingredients

1⅓ cups all-purpose flour
1 teaspoon baking powder
½ teaspoon salt
⅓ cup dried cherries
1 cup chopped walnuts
3 tablespoons lavender flowers
1 cup butter
1 cup cocoa
1¾ cups sugar
4 eggs
2 teaspoons vanilla extract
Icing sugar

Shopping List

All-purpose flour
Baking powder
Salt
Dried cherries
Chopped walnuts
Lavender flowers
Butter
Cocoa
Sugar
Eggs
Vanilla extract
Icing sugar

Tools and Equipment: Mixing bowl, microwave-safe baking dish, mixing spoon or flexible spatula for blending ingredients

Method

MAKE AHEAD

Preheat the toaster oven to 350 degrees F. Butter an 8-inch by 8-inch baking dish.

1.   In a bowl, stir together the flour, baking powder, salt, cherries, walnuts, and lavender flowers.

2.   Melt the butter in the microwave in a microwave-safe bowl. Stir in the cocoa. Blend in the sugar, eggs, and vanilla.

3.   Pour the dry ingredients into the wet ingredients and mix thoroughly.

4.   Pour the batter into the baking pan.

5.   Bake for 35 to 40 minutes or until done.

6.   Cool and dust with icing sugar.

Garnish suggestions:
Fresh cherries when available
Mint sprig if being served as a dessert

Beverages

About beverages

Some of my favorite summer beverages are the types served in spas, like water with cucumber and fruit-based iced teas. They are so refreshing and make water a pleasure to drink. We all need to drink so much water in the hot months to stay hydrated but it can easily become a little bit boring. Here are some recipes to make water interesting again.

Enjoy!

Cucumber Mint Water

Cool as a cucumber! Here's a cooling and refreshing drink to keep on hand for those sultry days that nearly finish you off.

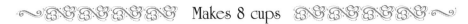 Makes 8 cups

Ingredients

1 English cucumber
7 or 8 sprigs of mint
8 cups of spring or filtered water

Shopping List

English cucumber
Mint

Method

1. Trim the ends of the cucumber, discarding the ends, then cut it into ½-inch slices. Put the cucumber slices into a water pitcher.

2. Add the mint, then the water. Gently stir. Let steep in the fridge for about 30 minutes before serving over ice.

Tools and Equipment: Knife, cutting board, pitcher, spoon for stirring

Three Citrus Water

Keep a jug of this in the fridge for a quick cool-me-down. For an extra-refreshing kick, use sparkling water for Three Citrus Fizz.

Makes approximately 9 cups

Ingredients

1 lemon
1 orange
1 lime
8 cups water approximately
Ice

Shopping List

1 lemon
1 orange
1 lime

Method

1. Wash the fruit well in cold water. Slice the lemon, orange, and lime into 4 or 5 slices each.

2. Put the slices of fruit in a pitcher and fill halfway with water, about 8 cups or you can experiment with the ratio of water to slices all summer long to find your favorite mix. Let it steep in the fridge for 30 minutes.

3. When ready to serve, fill the rest of the jug with ice and water. Stir to mix in the fruit slices.

Tools and Equipment: Knife, cutting board, pitcher, spoon for stirring

Lemon Cherry Iced Tea

*The tartness of the lemon and the sweetness of the cherries
balance each other for a refreshing summer beverage.*

 Makes about 8 cups

Ingredients

7 cups water
Lemon-flavored tea (4 tea bags)
Ice cubes, about 2 cups
1 lemon, sliced thin
½ cup frozen cherries

Shopping List

Lemon-flavored tea bags
Lemon
Frozen cherries

Method

1.   Boil the water to make the tea. Put the tea bags in a large teapot or large bowl and pour the boiled water over the tea bags. Let steep for about 5 minutes.

2.   Put the ice and lemon slices in a pitcher.

3.   Take out the tea bags and pour the tea slowly over the ice.

4.   Toss the frozen cherries into the pitcher and stir. Refrigerate for about 30 minutes before serving.

Tools and Equipment: Kettle, teapot or bowl, knife, cutting board, pitcher, spoon for stirring

Conversions and Measurement Equivalents

It's easy to keep these conversions and equivalents at your fingertips. Just copy the pages, cut out the boxes, laminate them, and attach a magnet to the back to stick on the fridge. You can also just laminate the entire page and keep it with your cookbooks. The lamination keeps the page clean while you're cooking.

Note: If you start with metric, continue with metric or your recipe will not turn out. Recipes with both measurements usually use 500 ml to "equal" 2 cups or 16 ounces, which will give you a bit more liquid than if you were using the imperial measures. All other ingredients are scaled to work with their relevant ratios so a metric recipe will usually produce a slightly larger volume overall.

The British tablespoon is 17.7 ml while the US tablespoon is 14.2 ml. In Britain, a cup is 10 ounces. The Australian tablespoon is 20 ml and in most Canadian recipes the tablespoon is 15 ml. In British, Australian, and often Canadian recipes, the Imperial pint, which is 20 fluid ounces, is used but US and sometimes Canadian recipes use the US pint of 16 fluid ounces.

ABBREVIATIONS

Tablespoon = T / Tbsp

Teaspoon = t / tsp

Cup = C

Ounce = oz

Milliliter = ml

Liter = L

Quart = qt

Pint = pt

Gallon = gal

Fluid = fl

Package = pkg

Pound = lb

Small = sm

Large = lg

Dry Measure Equivalents

1 T	= 3 t
1/16 cup	= 1 T
1/8 cup	= 2 T
1/6 cup	= 2 T + 2t
1/4 cup	= 4 T
1/3 cup	= 5 T + 1 t
3/8 cup	= 6 T
1/2 cup	= 8 T
2/3 cup	= 10 T + 2 t
3/4 cup	= 12 T
1 pinch	= 1/8 t or less
1 dash	= less than 1/4 t
1 teaspoon	= 60 drops
16 oz	= 1 pound
1 stick butter	= 1/2 cup

Measurement Equivalents - US

Cup	fl oz	Tbsp	tsp	ml
1/16 C	.5 oz	1 Tbsp	3 tsp	15 ml
1/8 C	1 oz	2 Tbsp	6 tsp	30 ml
1/4 C	2 oz	4 Tbsp	12 tsp	59 ml
1/3 C	3 oz	5 Tbsp	16 tsp	79 ml
1/2 C	4 oz	8 Tbsp	24 tsp	118 ml
2/3 C	5 oz	11 Tbsp	32 tsp	158 ml
3/4 C	6 oz	12 Tbsp	35 tsp	177 ml
1 C	8 oz	16 Tbsp	48 tsp	237 ml
2 C	16 oz	32 Tbsp		474 ml
4 C	32 oz	64 Tbsp		946 ml
16 C	128 oz			

Liquid Measure Equivalents - US

fl. oz	cup	pint	quart	liter	gallon
128	16	8	4	3.75	1
34	4.23	2.11	1.06	1	.26
32	4	2	1	.95	.25
16	2	1	.5	.47	.13
8	1	.5	.25	.24	.06

Liquid Metric/Imperial/US Cups/ US Pints

Metric (ml/L)	Imperial (fl.oz/pts)	US Cups	US Pints
30 ml	1 fl. oz	⅛	
60 ml	2 fl. oz	¼	
90 ml	3 fl. oz		
120 ml	4 fl. oz	½	¼ US pt
150 ml	5 fl. oz / ¼pt		
180 ml	6 fl. oz	¾	
210 ml	7 fl. oz		
240 ml	8 fl. oz	1	½ US pt
270 ml	9 fl. oz		
300 ml	10 fl. oz / ½ pt	1 ¼	
330 ml	11 fl. oz		
360 ml	12 fl. oz	1 ½	¾ US pt
390 ml	13 fl. oz		
420 ml	14 fl. oz	1 ¾	
450 ml	15 fl. oz / ¾ pt		
480 ml	16 fl. oz	2	1 US pt
600 ml	20 fl. oz / 1 pt	2 ½	
960 ml	32 fl. oz	4	
1.1 L	40 fl. oz / 2 pts	5	

Weight

Metric (grams, kg)	Imperial (oz, lb)
25 g	1 oz
50 g	2 oz
75 g	3 oz
100 g	4 oz = ¼ lb
125 g	4½ oz
150 g	5⅓ oz
175 g	6 oz
200 g	7 oz
225 g	8 oz = ½ lb
250 g	9 oz
275 g	10 oz
300 g	11 oz
325 g	11½ oz = ¾ lb
350 g	12⅓ oz
375 g	13 oz
400 g	14 oz
425 g	15 oz
450 g	16 oz = 1 lb
675 g	22 oz = 1½ lb
1 kg	2.2 lb
1.2 kg	2½ lb
1.3 kg	3 lb
1.8 kg	4 lb
2.2 kg	5 lb

Oven Temperature Equivalents

Gas Mark	Fahrenheit	Celsius	Informal
¼	225	110	
½	250	130	cool/very slow
1	275	140	
2	300	150	warm/slow
3	325	170	
4	350	180	moderate
5	375	190	moderately hot
6	400	200	
7	425	220	hot
8	450	230	very hot
9	475	245	extremely hot
10	500	260	

INDEX

Angel Food Cake with Fruit Compote and Custard 80

Apples with Vanilla and Lavender 72

apples: Angel Food Cake with Fruit Compote and Custard 80
Apples with Vanilla and Lavender 72
Chicken with Dijon Vinaigrette, Fennel, and Apples, with Thyme Potatoes 56

artichokes: Pasta with Zucchini, Artichokes, and Capers with Parmesan 52

asparagus: Roasted Asparagus Spears Wrapped with Prosciutto with Herbed Risotto and Mixed Baby Greens with Mandarin and Pistachios 58

Balsamic Onions 66

Bean Salad with White Balsamic Vinaigrette 60

beverages: Cucumber Mint Water 86
Lemon Cherry Iced Tea 88
Orange and Strawberry Juice 28
Three Citrus Water 87

Blueberry Lemon Pie with Custard 78

cheese: Chicken and Brie Sandwiches with Balsamic Onions 38
Croissants with Strawberries, Mascarpone, and Almonds 30
Fancy Tuna Melt with Fine Herbs Mayonnaise and Swiss Cheese 44
Ham and Parmesan Sandwiches with Herbed Mayonnaise and Apricot Jam 62
Pasta with Zucchini, Artichokes, and Capers with Parmesan 52
Smoked Salmon, Brie, and Balsamic Portobello Mushroom Baguette 42
Smoked Salmon, Summer Fruits, Mascarpone Cheese, and Croissant Plate 32

chicken: Chicken and Brie Sandwiches with Balsamic Onions 38
Chicken with Dijon Vinaigrette, Fennel, and Apples, with Thyme Potatoes 56
Gourmet Dinner Salad with Rotisserie Chicken or Smoked Salmon 50
Mango Coconut Chicken 54

Chicken and Brie Sandwiches with Balsamic Onions 38

Chicken with Dijon Vinaigrette, Fennel, and Apples, with Thyme Potatoes 56

chickpeas: Bean Salad with White Balsamic Vinaigrette 60

chocolate: Lavender Brownies with Cherries 82

Citrus Mango Almond Salad 26

coconut: Mango Coconut Chicken 54

coffee: Parisian Breakfast 34
What Is Café au Lait? 35

Cold Melon Soup with Port 74

Croissants with Strawberries, Mascarpone, and Almonds 30

Cucumber Mint Water 86

dressings and mayos: Dijon Vinaigrette 56
Fine Herbs Mayonnaise 45
Herbed Mayonnaise 62
White Balsamic Vinaigrette 60
About dressings 57

drinks, see beverages

energy-saving tips: 4, 7

equipment, list of: 10

Fancy Tuna Melt with Fine Herbs Mayonnaise and Swiss Cheese 44

fennel: Chicken with Dijon Vinaigrette, Fennel, and Apples, with Thyme Potatoes 56

flavor: The Rule of Four Flavors 22

Gourmet Dinner Salad with Rotisserie Chicken or Smoked Salmon 50

Ham and Parmesan Sandwiches with Herbed Mayonnaise and Apricot Jam 62

lavender: Apples with Vanilla and Lavender 72
Lavender Brownies with Cherries 82

Lavender Brownies with Cherries 82

Lemon Cherry Iced Tea 88

lemons: Blueberry Lemon Pie with Custard 78
Lemon Cherry Iced Tea 88
Three Citrus Water 87

make-ahead recipes: 23
Apples with Vanilla and Lavender 72
Balsamic Onions 66
Bean Salad with White Balsamic Vinaigrette 60
Blueberry Lemon Pie with Custard 78
Lavender Brownies with Cherries 82
Roasted Asparagus Spears Wrapped with Prosciutto with Herbed Risotto and Mixed Baby Greens with Mandarin and Pistachios 58
Smoked Salmon, Brie, and Balsamic Portobello Mushroom Baguette 42
Summer Mangos with Nutmeg 70
Toaster Oven Roasted Balsamic Tomatoes 64

Mango Coconut Chicken 54

mangos: Citrus Mango Almond Salad 26
Mango Coconut Chicken 54
Simple Summer Salad with Fruit 46
Summer Mangos with Nutmeg 70
mayonnaise: see dressings and mayos
melon: Cold Melon Soup with Port 74
Simple Salad 40
Simple Summer Salad with Fruit 46
Smoked Salmon, Summer Fruits,
Mascarpone Cheese, and Croissant Plate 32
microwaves: 10-11
mushrooms: Smoked Salmon, Brie, and
Balsamic Portobello Mushroom Baguette 42

No-Cook Cooking, about: 4, 7
nuts: Citrus Mango Almond Salad 26
Croissants with Strawberries, Mascarpone,
and Almonds 30

onions: Balsamic Onions 66
Chicken and Brie Sandwiches with
Balsamic Onions 38
Orange and Strawberry Juice 28
oranges: Citrus Mango Almond Salad 26
Orange and Strawberry Juice 28
Three Citrus Water 87
outdoor eating: 5, 16-17

pantry basics: 12-13
Parisian Breakfast 34
Pasta with Zucchini, Artichokes, and Capers
with Parmesan 52
pastry: Blueberry Lemon Pie with Custard 78
Croissants with Strawberries, Mascarpone,
and Almonds 30
Parisian Breakfast 34
Smoked Salmon, Summer Fruits,
Mascarpone Cheese, and Croissant Plate 32
Blind baking 79
Where to find chocolate croissants 35
potatoes: Chicken with Dijon Vinaigrette,
Fennel, and Apples, with Thyme
Potatoes 56
prosciutto: Roasted Asparagus Spears
Wrapped with Prosciutto with Herbed
Risotto and Mixed Baby Greens with
Mandarin and Pistachios 58

rice: Roasted Asparagus Spears Wrapped
with Prosciutto with Herbed Risotto and
Mixed Baby Greens with Mandarin and
Pistachios 58
Roasted Asparagus Spears Wrapped with
Prosciutto with Herbed Risotto and Mixed
Baby Greens with Mandarin and
Pistachios 58

salads: Bean Salad with White Balsamic
Vinaigrette 60
Citrus Mango Almond Salad 26
Gourmet Dinner Salad with Rotisserie
Chicken or Smoked Salmon 50
Simple Salad 40
Simple Summer Salad with Fruit 46
salmon: Gourmet Dinner Salad with
Rotisserie Chicken or Smoked Salmon 50
Smoked Salmon, Brie, and Balsamic
Portobello Mushroom Baguette 42
Smoked Salmon, Summer Fruits,
Mascarpone Cheese, and Croissant Plate 32
sandwiches: Chicken and Brie Sandwiches
with Balsamic Onions 38
Fancy Tuna Melt with Fine Herbs
Mayonnaise and Swiss Cheese 44
Ham and Parmesan Sandwiches with
Herbed Mayonnaise and Apricot Jam 62
Smoked Salmon, Brie, and Balsamic
Portobello Mushroom Baguette 42
shopping tips: 14-15
shortcuts: 5
Simple Salad 40
Simple Summer Salad with Fruit 46
Smoked Salmon, Brie, and Balsamic Portobello
Mushroom Baguette 42
Smoked Salmon, Summer Fruits, Mascarpone
Cheese, and Croissant Plate 32
soup: Cold Melon Soup with Port 74
Strawberries and Cream Soup 76
strawberries: Croissants with Strawberries,
Mascarpone, and Almonds 30
Orange and Strawberry Juice 28
Simple Salad 40
Simple Summer Salad with Fruit 46
Smoked Salmon, Summer Fruits,
Mascarpone Cheese, and Croissant Plate 32
Strawberries and Cream Soup 76
Fanning a Strawberry 33
Strawberries and Cream Soup 76
Summer Mangos with Nutmeg 70

Three Citrus Water 87
Toaster Oven Roasted Balsamic Tomatoes 64
tomatoes: Toaster Oven Roasted Balsamic
Tomatoes 64
tuna: Fancy Tuna Melt with Fine Herbs
Mayonnaise and Swiss Cheese 44

vanilla: Apples with Vanilla and Lavender 72
How to remove vanilla seeds 27

zucchini: Pasta with Zucchini, Artichokes, and
Capers with Parmesan 52